THE GHOST SONATA

August Strindberg

translated from the Swedish by Laurence Senelick

BROADWAY PLAY PUBLISHING INC
224 E 62nd St, NY, NY 10065
info@broadwayplaypub.com
www.broadwayplaypub.com

THE GHOST SONATA

cover art: *Die Toteninsel* by Arnold Böcklin

I S B N: 978-0-88145-637-0
First printing: November 2015

Book design: Marie Donovan
Page make-up: Adobe InDesign
Typeface: Palatino
Printed and bound in the U S A

TRANSLATOR'S NOTE

August Strindberg's SPÖKSONATEN was written in
1907 and first produced at Stockholm's Intima Teatern,
which he co-founded, on 21 January 1908. It followed a
typically fraught period in his life. It had seen a divorce
from his third wife, the actress Harriet Bosse; a public
feud with Stockholm society; and the onset of stomach
cancer. He also felt oppressed by having regularly to
hire and fire incompetent domestics.

THE GHOST SONATA is the third of Strindberg's
Chamber Plays, whose title comes from Beethoven's
Piano Sonata no. 17 in D minor (op. 31, no. 2), the so-
called *Geister-sonata*. Some critics have tried to discern
a musical structure to the play, but the notion of three
acts representing three movements is based on a
misconception. Strindberg did not intend act breaks
(English versions invariably divide the play into three
acts) but sprinkled the dialogue with asterisks. Even
they are inconsistent as guides to "French scenes".
I believe he wanted the action to be continuous,
characteristic of a dream play. It can be performed
without breaks in about an hour and forty-five minutes
and is far more powerful when staged in that way.

In his later years Strindberg believed in a syncretic
religion of his own devising, an amalgam of
elements from Christianity, Buddhism, Hinduism,
Swedenborgianism and Eduard von Hartmann's
pessimism. In his belief system, life on earth is a kind

of hell or at best purgatory, full of falsehood and façades; the more embroiled one is in it the more wicked and tormented one becomes. Hence the Hummel family are not vampires in the traditional sense: they are hyperactive yet sterile life-lovers who they have to suck life from others. (Strindberg originally intended the Young Lady, Hummel's daughter, to have cancer of the womb, thus incapable of producing life.) The human condition devoutly to be wished is a Nirvana-like transcendence of worldly concerns.

In Swedish, Strindberg's play is terse in its phrasing, stylistically uneven, sometimes banal but often rising to the level of lyrical incantation. Late in his career, he had developed a style that mixed the poetic and Biblical with colloquialism and journalese. In this translation, I have tried to preserve the strangeness of the dialogue by retaining Strindberg's sentence order and using, whenever possible, words of Germanic, rather than Latinate, origin. I have been careful not to iron out the illogical or inconsistent wrinkles, but to let the play remain as enigmatic in translation as it is in the original.

CHARACTERS

THE OLD MAN, *Chairman Hummel*
THE STUDENT, *Arkenholz*
THE MILKMAID, *an apparition*
THE DOORMAN'*s wife*
THE DEAD MAN, *a consul*
THE BLACK-CLAD LADY, *daughter of* THE DEAD MAN *and*
    THE DOORMAN'S WIFE
THE COLONEL
THE MUMMY, THE COLONEL'*s wife*
THE DAUGHTER, *or rather,* THE OLD MAN'S DAUGHTER
THE TITLED GENT, *alias Baron Skanskorg; engaged to* THE
    DOORMAN'S WIFE'S DAUGHTER
JOHANSSON, *servant to* THE OLD MAN
BENGTSSON, *footman to* THE COLONEL
THE FIANCÉE, *once engaged to* THE OLD MAN, *a white-
    haired old lady*
THE COOK
A HOUSEMAID
BEGGARS

(The ground floor and first story façade of an up-to-date apartment building, but only a corner of the building, for the ground floor ends in a round parlor. Above it, on the upper story, are a balcony and a flagpole.)

(Through the open window to this round parlor, when its roller-blinds are drawn up, one can see a white marble statue of a young woman, surrounded by palms, starkly lit by the sun's rays. In the windows left are to be seen pots of hyacinths [blue, white, pink].)

(On the balcony railing in the corner above are to be seen a blue silk bedspread and two white pillows. The windows to the left are draped in white sheets [Translator's note: A sign of mourning in Sweden]. It is a clear Sunday morning.)

(Downstage, before the façade, stands a green bench.)

(Down right, a public drinking fountain; down left, an advertising kiosk.)

(Up left is the entrance door, revealing a staircase, steps of white marble, the bannister of mahogany and brass; on either side of the door on the sidewalk stand laurels in tubs.)

(The corner of the round parlor also faces a side-street which seems to go upstage.)

(Left of the entrance door is a ground-floor window with a one-way mirror reflecting the street to the interior.)

(As the curtain rises, the bells of several distant churches are ringing.)

(The doors of the building are open; a black-clad woman stands motionless on the steps.)

(The DOORMAN'S WIFE *is sweeping the front hall; then she polishes the brass on the door; then she waters her laurels.)*

(In a wheelchair by the kiosk sits the OLD MAN, *reading the newspaper; he has white hair and beard and eyeglasses.)*

(The MILKMAID *enters from the corner with bottles in a wire basket; she is dressed for summer, with brown shoes, black stockings, and a white bonnet; takes off the bonnet and hangs it on the fountain; wipes the sweat from her brow; drinks a sip from the dipper; washes her hands; tidies her hair, using the reflection in the water.)*

(A steamboat bell rings, and the bass notes of an organ in a nearby church now and again pierce the stillness.)

(After a few moments' stillness, when the MILKMAID *has finished her toilette, the* STUDENT *enters left, unshaven and unkempt. He goes right to the fountain.)*

(Pause)

STUDENT: May I borrow the dipper?

*(*MILKMAID *hugs the dipper to herself.)*

STUDENT: Aren't you through yet?

*(*MILKMAID *stares at him in horror.)*

OLD MAN: *(To himself)* Who is he talking to? —I see nothing! —Is he crazy? *(Continues to look at them in great wonderment.)*

STUDENT: What're you staring at? Do I look so terrible? —True, I haven't slept all night, and you think, naturally, that I was out boozing…

*(*MILKMAID *as before)*

STUDENT: Swilling rum punch, right? —Do I smell of punch?

*(*MILKMAID *as before)*

STUDENT: I'm unshaven, I know it… Give me a drink of water, girl, for I've earned it! *(Pause)* Well! Then

I'll have to stop and tell you that I've been bandaging wounds and tending to the sick all night long; the fact is, I was on the spot when that house caved in last night... Now you know.

(MILKMAID *rinses out the dipper and gives* STUDENT *a drink.*)

STUDENT: Thanks!

(MILKMAID *motionless*)

STUDENT: *(Slowly)* Will you do me a big favor? *(Pause)* The thing is, my eyes are inflamed, as you can see, but my hands have touched sores and the like; that's why I can't risk putting them near my eyes... Will you take my clean handkerchief, soak it in fresh water and bathe my poor eyes? —Will you? —Will you be the good Samaritan?

(MILKMAID *hesitates, but does as* STUDENT *asks.*)

STUDENT: Thanks, friend! *(He takes out his purse.)*

(MILKMAID *makes a deprecating gesture.*)

STUDENT: Forgive my thoughtlessness, but I'm in a daze...

OLD MAN: *(To the* STUDENT*)* Excuse my intrusion, but I heard you say you were at the accident last night... I've been sitting here reading about it in the paper...

STUDENT: Is it in there already?

OLD MAN: Yes, the whole business! And your portrait with it, though they regret that they were unable to find out the daring student's name...

STUDENT: *(Glances at the paper)* That so? That's me! How 'bout that!

OLD MAN: Who was that you were talking to just now?

STUDENT: Didn't you see?

(Pause)

OLD MAN: Is it impertinent to ask—might I inquire—
your esteemed name?

STUDENT: What difference would it make? I'm not after
publicity—once a man gets praised, the carping starts
right in—the art of slander has made such progress—
anyway, I ask no reward…

OLD MAN: Wealthy, I suppose?

STUDENT: Not at all…quite the contrary! I'm broke.

OLD MAN: Listen here…I think I've heard your
voice…I had a friend in my youth who couldn't say
window, instead he always said "winder" —I never
met but one person who pronounced it that way and
he was that one— Can it be that you're related to the
wholesaler Arkenholz?

STUDENT: He was my father.

OLD MAN: Wondrous are the ways of fate… I saw you
when a toddler, in extremely harsh conditions…

STUDENT: Yes, I learned I was born into the world in
the midst of a bankruptcy…

OLD MAN: Absolutely right!

STUDENT: Might I ask your name?

OLD MAN: I am Chairman Hummel…

STUDENT: You're the one…? Then I remember…

OLD MAN: You've often heard my name mentioned in
your family?

STUDENT: Yes!

OLD MAN: And maybe mentioned with a certain
aversion?

(STUDENT *keeps silent.*)

OLD MAN: Yeah, I can imagine! —No doubt it was said
that I was the one who ruined your father? —All who

ruin themselves through stupid speculations think themselves ruined by those they couldn't cheat. *(Pause)* Now the fact of the matter is that your father robbed me of seventeen thousand crowns, the bulk of my savings at that time.

STUDENT: It's funny how a story can be told in two so different ways.

OLD MAN: Surely you don't think I've been telling untruths?

STUDENT: What should I think? My father didn't lie!

OLD MAN: That's so true, a father never lies…but I am a father too, so it follows…

STUDENT: What are you getting at?

OLD MAN: I rescued your father from distress, and he repaid me with all the hideous hatred a debt of gratitude breeds…he taught his family to speak ill of me.

STUDENT: Perhaps you made him ungrateful by poisoning the help with needless humiliations…

OLD MAN: All help is humiliating, sir.

STUDENT: What do you want from me?

OLD MAN: I'm not after money; but if you would do me a small service, I would be well repaid. Now, you see that I'm crippled, some say it's my own fault, others blame my parents, personally I think it is life itself with its ambushes; for in avoiding one of its snares, a man walks right into another. Nevertheless, I cannot spring up and down stairs, can't ring doorbells, that's why I say to you: help me!

STUDENT: What can I do?

OLD MAN: The first thing is, give my chair a shove, so that I can read the posters; I want to see what's playing this evening…

STUDENT: *(Shoving the wheelchair)* Haven't you a servant?

OLD MAN: Yeah, but he's gone on an errand…coming straight back…might you be a medical student?

STUDENT: No, I'm studying languages, but for the rest I don't know what I want to be…

OLD MAN: Hoho! —How're your math skills?

STUDENT: All right, so-so.

OLD MAN: Bully for you!—Would you like to have a position perhaps?

STUDENT: Sure, why not?

OLD MAN: Good. *(Reading the poster.)* They're doing *The Valkyrie* at the matinee… So the Colonel'll be there with his daughter, and since he always sits at the far end of Row Six, I'll put you beside him… Will you go into the phone booth there and order a ticket for row six, seat number 82?

STUDENT: Am I to go to the opera this afternoon?

OLD MAN: Yes! And if you obey me, you'll fare very nicely. I want you to be happy, rich and honored; your debut yesterday as the knight in shining armor will make you famous by tomorrow and your name will be a valuable commodity.

STUDENT: *(Goes to the phone booth)* This might be an amusing adventure!..

OLD MAN: Are you a sportsman?

STUDENT: Yes, to my bad luck…

OLD MAN: Then we shall change your luck! —Now make the call! *(He reads his paper.)*

(The BLACK-CLAD LADY *has come out on the sidewalk and talks to the* DOORMAN'S WIFE; *the* OLD MAN *listens, but the audience hears nothing.)*

(STUDENT *re-enters.*)

OLD MAN: Is it set?

STUDENT: It's done.

OLD MAN: You see that house there?

STUDENT: I was just observing it…I walked by here yesterday, as the sun was shining on the window panes—and, picturing to myself all the beauty and luxury to be found inside—I said to my companion, "What would it be like to own a flat in there, four flights up, with a beautiful wife, two pretty little children, and an annuity of twenty thousand crowns…"

OLD MAN: That's what you said? That's what you said? Look at that! I love that house too.

STUDENT: You speculate in houses?

OLD MAN: N-yes! But not in the way you mean…

STUDENT: You know the people who live there?

OLD MAN: All of 'em. At my age a man knows all mankind, their fathers and forefathers, and a man is always related to them in some way—I am now eighty—but no one knows me rightly. —I take an interest in men's fates…

(*The roller-blinds in the round parlor are drawn up; the* COLONEL *appears inside, in civilian clothes; after looking at the barometer, he goes back into the room and stands in front of the marble statue.*)

OLD MAN: Yes, there is the Colonel, whom you will sit beside this afternoon…

STUDENT: Is that—the Colonel? I can't make sense of any of this, but it's like a fairy tale…

OLD MAN: The whole of my life is like a book of fairy tales, sir; but although the stories are dissimilar, they hang together by the same thread, and the main theme recurs regularly.

STUDENT: Who is that marble statue inside?

OLD MAN: That's his wife, of course…

STUDENT: Was she so lovely then?

OLD MAN: Ha yes! Yes!

STUDENT: Tell me!

OLD MAN: We can't judge other people, dear boy!— What if I were to tell you that she walked out, that he slugged her, that she came back again, remarried him and that *she* now sits in there like a mummy, and worships her own statue, would you think I was crazy?

STUDENT: I don't understand.

OLD MAN: I thought not! —Then we have the hyacinth window. There lives his daughter…she's out riding, but she'll come straight home.

STUDENT: Who is the black-clad lady, who's talking to the doorman's wife there?

OLD MAN: Yes, this is a little involved, but it's connected with the dead man up there where you see the white sheets…

STUDENT: Yes, who was he?

OLD MAN: He was a man, like us, but he was known mostly for his vanity… If you were a Sunday's child, you should soon see him come out the door to admire the consulate flag at half-mast. —He was appointed Consul, and was fond of coronets, lions, plumed hats and colored ribbons.

STUDENT: You spoke of a Sunday's child—actually I learned I was born on a Sunday.

OLD MAN: No! were you...? I might have known...I see it from the color of your eyes...but then you can see what others do not see, haven't you noticed this?

STUDENT: I don't know what others see, but sometimes...yes, men don't talk about such things!

OLD MAN: I was almost sure of it! But you can tell me... For I—understand such things...

STUDENT: For instance, yesterday...I was drawn to that nondescript street where the house later caved in... I came down it and stood in front of a building that I had never seen before... Then I noticed a crack in the wall; heard how the floor boards cracked; I sprang forward and grabbed a child walking beside the wall... The next second the house caved in...I was safe, but in my arms, where I thought I held the child, I found nothing...

OLD MAN: Well, I must say...I thought as much... Fill me in on something: why were you gesticulating just now at the fountain? And why were you talking to yourself?

STUDENT: Didn't you see the milkmaid I was talking to?

OLD MAN: (Terrified) Milkmaid?

STUDENT: Yes, sure, the one who gave me the dipper.

OLD MAN: That so? That's how things stand? ...Oh well, I may not have the power to see, but I have other powers...

(Now a WHITE-HAIRED WOMAN appears and sits down at the window with the mirror reflecting the street.)

OLD MAN: See that old woman in the window! You see her? Good! That was my fiancée once, sixty years ago... I was twenty. —Don't be afraid, she doesn't know me now. We see one other every day, but without the slightest effect on me, although we plighted each other everlasting troth once; everlasting!

STUDENT: How reckless you were in the old days! We never tell such things to our girls now.

OLD MAN: Forgive us, young man, we didn't know any better!—But can you see that that old woman was young and beautiful?

STUDENT: It doesn't show. Yeah, she has a pretty look about her, her eyes I can't see!

(DOORMAN'S WIFE *comes out with a basket and strews spruce twigs [translators note: used in Sweden for funeral wreaths].*)

OLD MAN: The doorman's wife, ah yes!—That lady in black there is her daughter by the dead man, and that's why her husband got the job as doorman... But the dark lady has a suitor, he is a titled gent, and intends to get rich; he's counting on a divorce from his wife, of course, who is giving him a mansion just to be rid of him. The titled suitor is a son-in-law of the dead man, and you see his bedclothes being aired up there on the balcony... It is involved, I must say!

STUDENT: It's awfully involved!

OLD MAN: Yeah, that it is, inside and out, although at first it looks simple.

STUDENT: But who was this dead man?

OLD MAN: You asked me before, and I answered: could you see round the corner, where the service stairs are, you'd spot a bunch of the poor whom he helped... when he felt like it...

STUDENT: He was a charitable man then?

OLD MAN: Yes...at times.

STUDENT: Not always?

OLD MAN: Neh! ...That's what people are like! —Listen here, sir, move my chair a bit, so I get in the sun, I'm freezing so awfully: when you never get to move around, the blood curdles—I shall die soon enough, I know it, but beforehand I have a bit to do—take my hand, so you'll feel how cold I am.

STUDENT: This is not normal! *(Recoils)*

OLD MAN: Don't leave me, I'm tired, I'm lonely, but I haven't always been this way, you understand; I have an endlessly long life behind me—endlessly—I've made men unhappy and men have made me unhappy, the one cancels out the other—but before I die I want to see you happy... Our fates are intertwined through your father and other things...

STUDENT: Do let go of my hand, you're draining my strength, you're freezing me, what do you want?

OLD MAN: Patience, and you shall see and understand... Here comes the young lady...

STUDENT: The Colonel's daughter?

OLD MAN: Yes! Daughter! Look at her! —Have you ever seen such a masterpiece?

STUDENT: She's like the marble statue in there...

OLD MAN: The one of her mother?

STUDENT: You're right— Never saw I such a woman of woman born. —"Blessed the man who leads her to the altar and home!"

OLD MAN: You can see that! —Not everyone perceives her beauty... Well, so it is written!

(YOUNG LADY *enters left in a modern English riding habit, crosses slowly, without looking at anyone, to the house door. There she stops and says a few words to the* DOORMAN'S WIFE, *then enters the house.*)

STUDENT: *(His hands over his eyes)*

OLD MAN: You crying?

STUDENT: Faced with hopelessness, all you can do is despair!

OLD MAN: I can open doors and hearts, if only I find an arm to do my will... Serve me, and you shall prevail...

STUDENT: Is this some sort of pact? Am I to sell my soul?

OLD MAN: Sell nothing! —Look here, I have *taken,* all my life, now I have a craving to give! Give! But no one will receive... I'm rich, mighty rich, but I have no heirs, yeah, one loafer who tortures the life out of me... Be a son to me, inherit while I live, enjoy existence so long as I can see it, if only at a distance.

STUDENT: What am I to do?

OLD MAN: Go and hear *The Valkyrie* first!

STUDENT: That is already settled—what else?

OLD MAN: This evening you shall be sitting in there in the round parlor!

STUDENT: How am I to get in there?

OLD MAN: By way of *The Valkyrie!*

STUDENT: Just why have you chosen me as your medium? Have you known me before?

OLD MAN: Yes, of course! I've had my eye on you a long while. But see there now, see on the balcony how the maid is hoisting the flag half-mast for the Consul... and now she is turning over the bedclothes... You see that blue bedspread? -- It was for two to sleep under, but now it is for one...

(YOUNG LADY *appears, in a change of clothes, to water the hyacinths in the window.*)

OLD MAN: That is *my* little girl, look at her, look! — She's talking to the blooms. Is she not herself like a blue hyacinth? ...She gives them drink, only plain water, and they transform the water into color and aroma...now comes the Colonel with the newspaper! —He shows her the caved-in house...now she points to your portrait! She's not indifferent...she reads about the exploit... think it's clouding up, what if it starts to rain, I'm sitting pretty here if Johansson doesn't come back soon...

(The sky clouds over and turns murky; the OLD WOMAN *at the mirror closes her window.)*

OLD MAN: Now my fiancée closes her window... seventy-nine years old...that mirror is the only mirror she owns, because she can't see herself it in, only the outside world and from two directions, but the world can see her, that she didn't think of... A lovely old woman, for all that...

(Now the DEAD MAN *in a shroud comes out of the front door.)*

STUDENT: Good Lord, what do I see?

OLD MAN: What do you see?

STUDENT: Don't *you* see, in the doorway, a dead man?

OLD MAN: I see nothing, but it's just what I expected! Tell me...

STUDENT: He goes out in the street...

(Pause)

(Now the DEAD MAN *turns his head and looks at the flag.)*

OLD MAN: What'd I tell you? He's come out to count the wreaths and read the condolence cards... Woe betide those who are missing!

STUDENT: Now he turns the corner...

OLD MAN: He will count the poor at the service stairs... The poor are so nice and decorative;

"Accompanied by the blessings of the crowd," yes, but no blessings from me!—Between you and me, he was a great con man!..

STUDENT: But charitable…

OLD MAN: A charitable con man, always looking forward to a handsome funeral… When he knew his end was nigh, he swindled the State out of fifty thousand crowns… now his daughter there is breaking up another woman's marriage and wondering about the inheritance… He, the scoundrel, hears every word we say, and he's more than welcome to it!—Here comes Johansson!

(JOHANSSON *enters left.*)

OLD MAN: Report!

(JOHANSSON *talks inaudibly.*)

OLD MAN: Aha, not at home? You are a fool!—And the telegram? —Nothing! …Go on!.. Six o'clock this evening? That's good! —A special edition? —His full name in it? —Student Arkenholz, born…parents… first rate…I think it's beginning to rain. Just what did he say? …Aha, aha! —He will not? —Well, he has to! —Here comes the Titled Gent! —Shove me round the corner, Johansson, so I can hear what the poor are saying… And, Arkenholz, wait for me here… understand? —Look sharp, look sharp!

JOHANSSON (*pushes the wheelchair around the corner*)

STUDENT: (*Stays behind and watches the* YOUNG LADY, *who is now raking soil in the flower pots.*)

TITLED GENT: (*Clad in mourning, addresses the* BLACK-CLAD LADY, *who walks along the sidewalk*) Yes, what can one do about it? —We must wait!

BLACK-CLAD LADY: I cannot wait!

TITLED GENT: Is that so? Go to the country then!

BLACK-CLAD LADY: I will not do that.

TITLED GENT: Come over here, others will hear what we're saying.

(They go over towards the advertising kiosk and carry on their conversation inaudibly.)

*

JOHANSSON: *(Enters right; to the* STUDENT*)* My master bids the gentleman, don't forget the other thing!

STUDENT: *(Slowly)* Listen here—tell me first: who is your master?

JOHANSSON: Yes! He's so many things, and he's been everything.

STUDENT: Is he sane?

JOHANSSON: Yes, what's *that* mean? He has all his life sought for a Sunday's child, so he claims, but that may not be true...

STUDENT: What's he want, is he greedy?

JOHANSSON: He wants to run things... All day long he rides around in his chariot like the god Thor...he looks at houses, tears them down, rips open streets, rebuilds markets, but he also breaks into houses; creeps in through the window, wreaks havoc with men's fates, kills his enemies and never forgives. —Can you imagine, sir, that that little paralytic was once a Don Juan, though he always lost his women?

STUDENT: They hardly go together, do they?

JOHANSSON: Yeah, he's so crafty that he got his women to go, when he tired of them... Nevertheless, now he's more like a horse thief at a slave market, he steals human beings, in many ways... Me he literally stole out of the hands of the Law...I had, you see, committed a, hm, blunder; that only he knew about; instead of turning me in, he made me his slave: I slave for my vittles, which are far from the best...

STUDENT: What's he want to do in this house?

JOHANSSON: Yes, look, that I won't say! It is so involved.

STUDENT: I think I'll get out of here...

JOHANSSON: See, the young lady has dropped her bracelet out the window...

(The YOUNG LADY *has dropped her bracelet out the open window.)*

*(*STUDENT *meekly steps forward, takes up the bracelet and hands it to the* YOUNG LADY, *who thanks him stiffly; the* STUDENT *goes back to* JOHANSSON.)*

JOHANSSON: Ah yes, the gent's thinking of going... It isn't as easy as you think once *he's* slipped the net over your head... And he fears nothing between heaven and earth... Yeah, one thing, or rather one person...

STUDENT: Wait now, maybe I know!

JOHANSSON: How can you know?

STUDENT: I can guess!— Is it...a little milkmaid he fears?

JOHANSSON: He always turns away when he meets a milk wagon... and he talks in his sleep, he was surely in Hamburg once...

STUDENT: Can you trust that man?

JOHANSSON: You can trust him—to do anything!

STUDENT: What's he doing around the corner now?

JOHANSSON: He listens to the poor... Sowing a little word, plucking out a grain of sand, until the house caves in... figuratively speaking... You see, I am an educated fellow and I used to be a bookseller... Are you going now?

STUDENT: I have a hard time being ungrateful… That man rescued my father once, and now he barely asks a little favor in return…

JOHANSSON: What is that?

STUDENT: I'm to go and see *The Valkyrie.*

JOHANSSON: That I don't understand… but he always has a new angle… See, now he's talking to the policeman…he always keeps in with the police, and uses them, inveigles them with schemes, binds them with false promises and prospects, while all the while he's pumping them. —You shall see, before nightfall he'll be received in the round parlor.

STUDENT: What does he want there? What's between him and the Colonel?

JOHANSSON: Yes… I suspect, but I don't know! You'll get to see for yourself, when you go there..

STUDENT: I'll never get in there…

JOHANSSON: That depends on you!—Go to *The Valkyrie!*

STUDENT: Is that the way?

JOHANSSON: Yes, if he said so! —Look at him, just look at him, in his battle wagon, drawn in triumph by the beggars who don't get a penny in return, barring a hint that something might be in store at his funeral!

OLD MAN: *(Enters, standing in his wheelchair, drawn by a* BEGGAR, *followed by others)* Hail the noble youth, who at risk of his own life rescued many in yesterday's disaster! Hail, Arkenholz!

(BEGGARS *bare their heads, but without cheering.)*

(YOUNG LADY *in the window waves her handkerchief.)*

(COLONEL *stares out his window.)*

(OLD WOMAN *stands at her window.)*

(MAID *on the balcony raises the flag to the top.)*

OLD MAN: Clap your hands, citizens, it is Sunday,
that's true, but the ass in the pit and the ear of grain
in the field grant us absolution (*Translator's note: a
reference to Luke 14:5*), and although I am not a Sunday's
child, I possess both the spirit of prophecy and the gift
of healing, for I have brought a drowning girl back
to life once...yes, it was in Hamburg, on a Sunday
morning like this...

*

(MILKMAID *enters, seen only by the* STUDENT *and the* OLD
MAN; *she stretches up her arms like someone drowning and
stares at the* OLD MAN)

OLD MAN: (*Sits down, then shrinks in terror*) Johansson,
carry me away! Fast! —Arkenholz, don't forget *The
Valkyrie!*

STUDENT: What is all this?

JOHANSSON: We shall see! We shall see!

*

(*Inside the round parlor, at back a white glazed tile stove
with pendulum clock and candelabrum; at right a hall with
a perspective into a green room with mahogany furniture;
at left stands the statue shaded by palms and able to be
concealed by curtains; up left the door to the hyacinth room.
There the* YOUNG LADY *sits and reads. The* COLONEL *can
be seen from the back as he sits and writes in the green room.
Bengtsson, a footman in livery, comes in from the hall with
Johansson in a tailcoat and white tie.*)

BENGTSSON: Now, Johansson, you'll serve, while I take
the wraps, you've handled this sort of thing before?

JOHANSSON: I go and push that battle wagon all day,
as you know, but at night I serve at parties, and it's
always been my dream to get into this here house...
They're peculiar folks, ain't they?

BENGTSSON: Ye-es, a little unusual, you might say.

JOHANSSON: Is this a musical soirée, or what?

BENGTSSON: It is the usual ghost supper, we call it. They drink tea, saying not a word, or else the Colonel talks by himself, and so they munch their cakes, all in unison, till it sounds like rats in a granary.

JOHANSSON: Why's it called a ghost supper?

BENGTSSON: They look like ghosts... And besides they've been holding it for twenty years, always the same people, saying the same things, or else keeping still for fear of letting slip something dreadful.

JOHANSSON: Isn't there a lady of the house too?

BENGTSSON: Oh yeah, but she's cracked; she sits in a closet, because her eyes can't take the light... She sits in there... (*Points to a wall-papered door in the wall*)

JOHANSSON: In there?

BENGTSSON: Ye-es, I just said they were a little unusual...

JOHANSSON: How does she look?

BENGTSSON: Like a mummy... Want to see her? (*He opens the papered door.*) Look, there she sits!

JOHANSSON: Holy cripes...

*

MUMMY: (*Gibbering*) Why does he open the door, haven't I said it must be shut?

BENGTSSON: (*Mimicking her gibbering*) Ta, ta, ta, ta. Little moppet must be good now, so she'll get something nice! —Pretty Polly!

MUMMY: (*Like a parrot*) Pretty Polly! Oh is Jakob there? Cuuutie!

BENGTSSON: She thinks she's a parrot, and it's just possible she is... *(To the* MUMMY*)* Polly, whistle a little for us!

(MUMMY *whistles.*)

JOHANSSON: I've seen plenty, but nothing like this!

BENGTSSON: You see, when a house gets old, it gets moldy, and when folks sit together a long time and torment each other, they go crazy. The lady of this house—hist, Polly! —This mummy has been sitting here for forty years—same husband, same furniture, same relatives, same friends... *(Shuts the door on the Mummy.)* And what's gone on in this house—that I hardly know... Look at this statue here... that's the mistress when young!

JOHANSSON: Ah, good grief!—Is that the mummy?

BENGTSSON: Yes! —It's enough to make you cry: —But this woman, through the power of imagination or something else, has taken on the characteristics of a chattering bird—she can't stand cripples and the sick... She can't stand her own daughter, because she's sick...

JOHANSSON: The young lady's sick?

BENGTSSON: Didn't you know that?

JOHANSSON: No!... And the Colonel, who is he?

BENGTSSON: That you shall see!

JOHANSSON *(Looking at the statue)* It's gruesome to think of... How old is the woman now?

BENGTSSON: That no one knows...but they tell that when she was thirty-five, she looked nineteen and she convinced the Colonel that she was... Here in this house... Do you know what that black Japanese screen is for, next to the chaise longue? —They call it the death screen and stand it in front when someone is about to die, same as in the hospital.

JOHANSSON: This is a horrible house... And the student longs for it as for paradise...

BENGTSSON: Which student? Oh yes, him! As is coming here tonight... The Colonel and the young lady met him at the opera, and were both charmed by him... Hm!... But now it's my turn to ask: who is your master? The boss-man in the wheelchair?

JOHANSSON: Yes! yes! —Is he coming here too?

BENGTSSON: He hasn't been invited.

JOHANSSON: Then he'll come uninvited! If need be...

*

(OLD MAN *enters the hall, in frock coat, top hat, on crutches. He sneaks forward and listens.*)

BENGTSSON: He's a downright thieving magpie, ain't he?

JOHANSSON: Fully-fledged!

BENGTSSON: He looks like the devil himself!

JOHANSSON: And he's surely a wizard too! —for he can go through locked doors...

OLD MAN: (*Coming forward, takes* JOHANSSON *by the ear*) Villain! —Take care! (*To* BENGTSSON) Announce my visit to the Colonel!

BENGTSSON: Yes, but he's expecting guests here...

OLD MAN: That I know! But my visit he sort of expects, though not eagerly...

BENGTSSON: That so! What's the name! Chairman Hummel!

OLD MAN: Exactly so!

(BENGTSSON *goes through the hall to the green room, where he closes the door.*)

OLD MAN: (*To* JOHANSSON) Vanish!

(JOHANSSON *hesitates.*)

OLD MAN: Vanish!

(JOHANSSON *vanishes down the hall.*)

OLD MAN: *(Inspects the room, stands before the statue in profound amazement.)* Amalia! …It is she! …She! *(He strays about the room and fingers things; adjusts his wig in the mirror; returns to the statue.)*

MUMMY: *(Inside the closet)* Pretty Polly!

OLD MAN: *(Taken aback)* What was that? Is there a parrot in the room? But I see nothing!

MUMMY: Is Jakob there?

OLD MAN: It's haunted!

MUMMY: Jakob!

OLD MAN: I'm gettin' spooked! …These are the secrets they've been keeping here in the house! *(He looks at a picture with his back turned to the closet.)* That is he…he!

MUMMY: *(Comes forward, behind the OLD MAN, and tugs on his wig)* Cuuu-tie! Is it Cuuu-tie?

OLD MAN: *(Leaps in the air)* Good God in heaven!—Who is that?

MUMMY: *(In a human voice)* Is that Jakob?

OLD MAN: My name is Jakob, indeed…

MUMMY: *(With emotion)* And my name is Amalia!

OLD MAN: No, no, no… Oh sweet Jesus…

MUMMY: This is how I look! Yes! —And once looked like *that*! Living is so educational—I live mostly in the closet, both to avoid seeing and to avoid being seen… But you, Jakob, what seek you here?

OLD MAN: My child! Our child…

MUMMY: She's sitting there.

OLD MAN: Where?

MUMMY: There, in the hyacinth room.

OLD MAN: *(Looking at the* YOUNG LADY*)* Yes, that is she! *(Pause)* What does her father say, I mean the Colonel? Your husband?

MUMMY: I was angry with him once and told him everything...

OLD MAN: We-ell?

MUMMY: He didn't believe me, only swore. "That's what all wives usually say when they want to murder their husbands." —It was a ghastly crime in any case. His whole life is pure counterfeit, his pedigree as well; I look at the list of nobility sometimes and think: That woman has a false birth certificate, like a kitchen maid, and that's punishable by a term in the reformatory.

OLD MAN: There are many who do that; I recall you had a forged birth date...

MUMMY: It was my mother who taught me to do it...I couldn't help it! ...But yours was the greater guilt in our crime...

OLD MAN: No, your husband caused that crime, for he took my fiancée from me! —Since I was born, I can never forgive until I have punished. —I took that as an imperative duty...and I still do so!

MUMMY: What seek you in this house? What do you want? How did you get in? —Is it about my daughter? Do you but touch her, so shall you die!

OLD MAN: I wish her well!

MUMMY: But you must spare her father!

OLD MAN: No!

MUMMY: Then you must die; in this room, behind that screen...

OLD MAN: Perhaps...but I can't let go once I bite...

MUMMY: You wish to marry her to the student: what for? He is nothing and has nothing.

OLD MAN: He'll be rich, through me!

MUMMY: Were you asked here this evening?

OLD MAN: No, but I've decided to ask myself to the ghost supper here!

MUMMY: Do you know who's coming?

OLD MAN: Not rightly.

MUMMY: The Baron...who lives upstairs, and whose father-in-law was buried at noon...

OLD MAN: He who is getting a divorce to marry the doorman's daughter... He, who was once your—lover!

MUMMY: And your former fiancée is coming, whom my husband seduced...

OLD MAN: A pretty assortment...

MUMMY: God, if we could die! *If only* we could die!

OLD MAN: Why do you go on meeting?

MUMMY: Crimes and secrets and guilt bind us together! —We have split up and gone our ways, so endlessly many times, but we're drawn together again...

OLD MAN: Now I think the Colonel is coming...

MUMMY: Then I'll go in to Adèle... *(Pause)* Jakob, think what you do! Spare him... *(Pause; she leaves.)*

COLONEL: *(Enters; cold, reserved)* Please take a seat!

(OLD MAN *slowly takes a seat.)*

(Pause)

COLONEL: *(Stares)* Are you the gentleman who wrote this letter?

OLD MAN: Yes!

(Pause)

COLONEL: I know that you have bought up all my outstanding I O Us, so it follows that I am in your clutches. What will you do now?

OLD MAN: I will have payment, but of another sort.

COLONEL: Of what sort?

OLD MAN: A mighty simple one—let us not talk of money—just tolerate me in your home, as a guest!

COLONEL: If you can be content with so little...

OLD MAN: Thanks!

COLONEL: Nothing else?

OLD MAN: Dismiss Bengtsson!

COLONEL: Why should I do that? My trusty old servant, who has been with me for a generation—who earned a national medal for faithful service. —Why should I do that?

OLD MAN: All those fine things are in your imagination— He is not what he seems to be!

COLONEL: And who is, precisely?

OLD MAN: *(Recoils)* True! But Bengtsson must go!

COLONEL: Will you give orders in my house?

OLD MAN: Yes! After all I own everything here— furniture, curtains, silverware, linen...and more!

COLONEL: What do you mean more?

OLD MAN: Everything! Everything you see I own, it is mine!

COLONEL: Very well, it is yours! But my noble coat of arms and my good name remain my own!

OLD MAN: No, not even that. *(Pause)* You are not a nobleman!

COLONEL: Shame on you!

OLD MAN: *(Takes out a piece of paper)* If you read this extract from the book of heraldry, you will see that the family whose name you bear died out a hundred years ago.

COLONEL: *(Reads)* I've certainly heard such rumors, but I inherited the name from my father... *(Reads)* It is right; you are right...I am not a nobleman! —Not even that! —So I take off my signet ring— That's true, it belongs to you... Be so good!

OLD MAN: *(putting on the ring)* Now let us continue!— You are not a colonel either!

COLONEL: I am not?

OLD MAN: No! You were appointed a provisional colonel in the American volunteers; but after the war in Cuba and reorganization of the army, all former commissions were revoked...

COLONEL: Is that true?

OLD MAN: *(Reaching into his pocket)* Want to read it?

COLONEL: No, that's not necessary! ...Who are you that has the right to sit and strip me bare like this?

OLD MAN: You shall see! But when it comes to stripping...do you know *who you* are?

COLONEL: Aren't you ashamed?

OLD MAN: Take off your wig and peer in the glass, just take out your teeth at the same time and shave off your moustache, let Bengtsson unlace your iron corset, so we can see if a certain servant, X Y Z, can recognize himself; he that scrounged scraps in a certain kitchen...

(COLONEL *reaches for the bell on the table.*)

OLD MAN: *(Forestalls him)* Don't touch that bell, don't call Bengtsson or I'll have him arrested... Here come your guests—keep calm now, so we can play our old roles for a while!

COLONEL: Who are you? I seem to know your glance and the sound of your voice...

OLD MAN: Ask not, be silent and but obey!

*

STUDENT: *(Enters, bows to the* COLONEL*)* Herr Colonel!

COLONEL: Welcome to my house, young man! Your noble conduct in the great disaster has brought your name to everyone's lips, and I deem it a great honor to welcome you to my home...

STUDENT: Herr Colonel, my lowly background... Your illustrious name and noble birth...

COLONEL: May I present Bachelor of Arts Arkenholz, Chairman Hummel... Would it please our student to step in and meet the ladies, I must conclude my chat with the Chairman...

(STUDENT *shown into the hyacinth room, where he remains visible, standing in bashful conversation with the* YOUNG LADY.)

COLONEL: A splendid young man: musical, a singer, writes poetry... Were he a nobleman and equal in birth, I should have nothing against... Yes...

OLD MAN: What's that?

COLONEL: My daughter...

OLD MAN: *Your* daughter! —By the way, why does she always sit in there?

COLONEL: She has to sit in the hyacinth room, when she is not out! It's a whim of hers... Here we have Miss Beate von Holsteinkrona...a charming creature... a lady on a pension sufficient for her standing and status...

OLD MAN: *(To himself)* My fiancée!

*

*(*FIANCÉE *enters, appears to be crazy.)*

COLONEL: Miss Holsteinkrona, Chairman Hummel…

*(*FIANCÉE *curtsies and sits.)*

*(*TITLED GENT *enters, mysteriously, clad in mourning, sits.)*

COLONEL: Baron Skanskorg…

OLD MAN: *(Aside, without rising)* I think he's the jewel thief… *(To the* COLONEL*)* Call in the Mummy, so the company may be complete…

COLONEL: *(In the doorway to the hyacinth room)* Polly!

*

MUMMY: *(Enters)* Cuuu-tie!

COLONEL: Shall the youngsters come in here too?

OLD MAN: No! Not the youngsters! They shall be spared…

(Now everyone sits in a circle, silent.)

COLONEL: Shall we have tea?

OLD MAN: What's the point of that! No one cares for tea, and therefore we shall not sit and pretend.

(Pause)

COLONEL: Shall we converse then?

OLD MAN: *(Slowly and with pauses)* Talk of the weather, which we feel, ask how we are, which we know. I prefer silence, to hear men thinking, and see their pasts; silence cannot hide anything…while words can; I read the other day that speech differences actually arose when savage peoples sought to hide their tribal secrets from others; so speeches are ciphers, and if one finds the key, one can understand all of the world's tongues; but that doesn't prevent secrets from being revealed without a key, and especially in the matter of vital proof of paternity; but proof before the courts, that's a bit different: two false witnesses constitute full proof, if they agree, but for the sort of expeditions I have in mind, no witnesses are needed, Nature herself has bestowed on mankind a sense of shame that seeks to hide what should be hidden; yet we glide into situations against our will, and occasions offer at times, when the most secret things must be revealed, when the mask is wrenched from the imposter, when the villain is unveiled...

(Pause; they all regard each other in silence.)

OLD MAN: So still you sit!

(Long silence)

OLD MAN: Here, for example, in this respectable house, in this lovely home, where beauty, culture and class unite...

(Long silence)

OLD MAN: All we who sit here, we know who we are... don't we? ...I don't have to say it...and you recognize me, though you pretend ignorance...in there sits my daughter, *mine*; you know that as well... She has lost the lust for life, without knowing why...but she is withering in this air breathing the crime, treachery and all sorts of falsehood... therefore I sought her a friend, in whose nearness she could discover the light and warmth of noble actions...

(Long silence)

OLD MAN: That was my mission in this house: to root out the weeds, expose crimes, balance the books, so that youth may begin anew in this home, which I present to them!

(Long silence)

OLD MAN: Now I grant you freedom to depart, each and every one in turn and order; anyone who stays I'll have arrested!

(Long silence)

OLD MAN: Hear how the clock ticks, the deathwatch beetle in the wall! You know what she says? "Time's up! Time's up!" —When it strikes in a little while, then your time is up, then you may go but not before. But it shudders first before it strikes! —Listen! How it warns: "The clock can strike". —I too can strike... *(He strikes the table with his crutch.)* You hear?

(Silence)

MUMMY: *(Crosses to the pendulum clock and stops it; then with grave concentration)* But I can stop time in its course—I can turn the past into nothing, undo what's been done; not with bribes, not with threats—but by suffering and repentance— *(Crosses to the* OLD MAN*)* We are wretched mortals, that we know; we have erred, we have transgressed, we like the rest; we are not what we seem, for at bottom we have a better self within us, for we deplore our failings; but that you Jakob Hummel with false name should sit in judgment, that shows you are worse than we wretches! You are no more what you seem to be than we are! —You are a thief of men's souls, for you stole mine once with false promises; you murdered the Consul who was buried today, you strangled him with debts and promissory notes; you have stolen the student by binding him with an imaginary debt of his father who never owed you a penny...

(OLD MAN *has attempted to rise and say a word, but has fallen back into a chair and crumpled up, crumpling more and more during what follows.)*

MUMMY: But I find one black spot in your life that I don't rightly know, just a hunch...I believe that

Bengtsson has the goods on that! (*Rings the bell on the table.*)

OLD MAN: No, not Bengtsson! Not him!

MUMMY: Aha, he knows it! (*Ringing again*)

(*Now the* MILKMAID *appears in the hallway, unseen by anyone except the* OLD MAN, *who is terrified; the* MILKMAID *vanishes when* BENGTSSON *enters.*)

MUMMY: Does Bengtsson know this gentleman?

BENGTSSON: Yeah, I know him and he knows me. Life as we know has its ups and downs, and I have served him, in times gone by he served me. He was then a scrounger in my kitchen for two whole years—since he had to be out by three o'clock, his meal was made ready by two o'clock, and the household had to eat the reheated leftovers of that there ox—but he also drank up the soup stock, which was then diluted with water—he sat there like a vampire and sucked all the marrow out of the house, so that we became like skeletons—and he said he'd put us in prison, when we called the cook a thief.
Later I met this man in Hamburg under an assumed name. Then he was a loan shark or bloodsucker, but there he was accused of tricking a girl out on to the ice to drown her, because she'd witnessed a crime he feared would be detected…

MUMMY: (*Passing her hand over the* OLD MAN's *face*) That is you! Now take out the IOU's and mortgages.

(JOHANSSON *appears in the hall doorway and watches the performance with great interest, for now he will be free of his thralldom.*)

OLD MAN: (*Takes out a bundle of papers and flings them on the table*)

MUMMY: (*Stroking the* OLD MAN's *back*) Polly! Is Jakob there?

OLD MAN: *(Like a parrot)* Jakob is there! —Cock-a-doodle-doo! Doodle-doo!

MUMMY: Can the clock strike?

OLD MAN: *(Clucking)* The clock can strike. *(Imitates a cuckoo clock.)* Cu-ckoo! Cu-ckoo, cu-ckoo!..

MUMMY: *(Opening the closet door)* Now the clock has struck! —Get up, go into the closet where I sat for twenty years and mourned our crime. —There hangs a rope inside that can remind you of the one you strangled the Consul with, and with which you planned to strangle your benefactor... Go!

(OLD MAN goes into the closet.)

MUMMY: *(Closes the door)* Bengtsson! Set the screen before him! Death screen!

(BENGTSSON sets the screen in front of the door.)

MUMMY: It is finished! —God have mercy on his soul!

EVERYONE: Amen!

(Long silence)

*

(In the hyacinth room, the YOUNG LADY appears with a harp on which she accompanies the STUDENT's recitation.)

(Song [after a prelude])

STUDENT: The sun saw I, to me it seemed
That I beheld the one concealed
And all his works were for man's joy,
blessèd be he that doeth good.
for deeds committed in thy wrath
cannot be recompensed by evil;
comfort him thou hast distrest
with thy goodness, thou shalt be repaid.
Naught to fear hath he who does no ill:
Goodness is innocence.

(*A room in somewhat bizarre style, oriental motif. Hyacinths of all colors throughout. On the tiled stove sits a great image of Buddha with a bulb in his lap, and from this the stem of a shallot [Allium ascanlonicum] shoots up, bearing its spherical clusters of white star-blooms.*)

(*Back right door to the round parlor; there the* COLONEL *and the* MUMMY *can be seen sitting idle and silent; even a portion of the death screen is visible. Left: door to pantry and kitchen.*)

(*The* STUDENT *and the* YOUNG LADY *[Adèle] at the table; she with a harp, he standing.*)

YOUNG LADY: Sing now for my blooms!

STUDENT: Is this your soul's bloom?

YOUNG LADY: It is my one and only! Do you love hyacinths?

STUDENT: I love them above all others, their virginal shape so slim and straight rises from the bulb, resting on water and sinking their pure white roots into the colorless liquid; I love their colors; the snow-white guiltless pure; the honey-gold luscious; the pink youthful; the red ripe; but above all others the blue, dewy blue, the deep-eyed, the steadfast... I loved them all, more than gold and pearls, have loved them since I was a child, have wondered at them, because they possess all the fine attributes I seek... And yet!..

YOUNG LADY: What?

STUDENT: My love is unrequited, for these lovely blossoms hate me...

YOUNG LADY: How so?

STUDENT: Their aroma, strong and pure as spring's first winds swept over melting snows, they bewilder my senses, deafen me, blind me, thrust me out of doors, shoot me full of poisoned arrows that make my heart ache and my head blaze! Know you this bloom's saga?

YOUNG LADY: Tell it!

STUDENT: But first its meaning. The bulb is the earth which rests on water or lies in mulch; then the stem shoots up, straight as the world's axis, and at the top sit the six-pointed star blooms.

YOUNG LADY: Stars over the earth! Oh, that is grand, where did you learn it, how did you see it?

STUDENT: Let me think—in your eyes! —It is therefore an image of the Cosmos... That's why Buddha sits with the bulb of the earth, brooding with his gaze as it grows outward and upward, transforming itself into a heaven. —This wretched earth shall be a heaven! For that, Buddha waits!

YOUNG LADY: Now I see— Isn't a snowflake also six-pointed like the hyacinth lily?

STUDENT: Right you are! —Snowflakes are falling stars...

YOUNG LADY: And the snowdrop is a snow star... grown out of snow.

STUDENT: But Sirius, the greatest and loveliest of the firmament's stars, is gold and red, it is the narcissus with its gold and red calix and six white beams...

YOUNG LADY: Have you seen the shallot in bloom?

STUDENT: Yes, indeed I have! —It bears its bloom in a ball, a cluster in the likeness of the heavenly globe bestrewn with white stars...

YOUNG LADY: Yes, God, how grand! Whose thought was that?

STUDENT: Thine!

YOUNG LADY: Thine!

STUDENT: Ours! —We have begot something together, we are wedded…

YOUNG LADY: Not yet…

STUDENT: What remains?

YOUNG LADY: Waiting, ordeals, patience!

STUDENT: Very well! Test me! *(Pause)* Tell me! Why do your parents sit in there so hushed, without saying a single word?

YOUNG LADY: Because they have nothing to say to one another, because neither believes what the other says. My father has put it this way: what is the point of speaking, neither of us can fool the other?

STUDENT: That is a ghastly thing to hear…

YOUNG LADY: Here comes the cook… Look at her, so coarse and fat she is…

STUDENT: What does she want?

YOUNG LADY: She will question me about dinner, I manage the household during my mother's sickness…

STUDENT: Must we bother about the cooking?

YOUNG LADY: Why, we must eat… Look at the cook, I cannot look at her…

STUDENT: Who is this monster?

YOUNG LADY: She belongs to the vampire family Hummel; she eats us up.

STUDENT: Why don't you dismiss her?

YOUNG LADY: She won't go! We have no power over her, we got her for our sins… Can't you see we are wasting away, consumed…

STUDENT: Don't you get any meat?

YOUNG LADY: Yeah, we get many dishes, but all the nourishment is gone… She boils our cuts of meat, gives

us gristle and water, while she herself drinks the stock;
...and if there is roast she boils out the marrow first,
eats the gravy, drinks the broth; all that she touches
loses its savor, it is as though she can suck through her
eyes; we get the dregs after she drinks the coffee, she
drains our wine bottles and fills them with water...

STUDENT: Throw her out!

YOUNG LADY: We cannot!

STUDENT: Why not?

YOUNG LADY: We don't know! She won't go! No one
has power over her—she has taken all the strength
from us!

STUDENT: May I throw her out?

YOUNG LADY: No! Things must be exactly as they
are! —Now she is here! She will ask me what I want
for dinner, I will answer this and that; she'll raise
objections, and so it is as she wills.

STUDENT: Let her decide for herself, then!

YOUNG LADY: That she will not do.

STUDENT: This is a wondrous strange house. It is
bewitched!

YOUNG LADY: Yes!—But now she turns away, when
she spies you!

*

COOK: *(In doorway)* Naw, that ain't why! *(She grins so
that she shows her teeth.)*

STUDENT: Out, woman!

COOK: When I please! *(Pause)* Now I please! *(Vanishes)*

YOUNG LADY: Don't get upset! —School yourself in
patience; she is one of the ordeals we endure here at

home! But we have a housemaid too! Whom we must
tidy up after!

STUDENT: Now I'm sinking! *Cor in æthere! (Latin: "Heart
in the sky!")* Sing!

YOUNG LADY: Wait!

STUDENT: Sing!

YOUNG LADY: Patience! —This room is called the room
of ordeals—it is beautiful to look upon, but is made up
of sheer imperfection...

STUDENT: Incredible, but a man can overlook that!
Beautiful it is, but a little cold. Why isn't the fire lit?

YOUNG LADY: Because the smoke comes in.

STUDENT: Can't the soot be cleared?

YOUNG LADY: That doesn't help! ...Do you see that
writing desk?

STUDENT: Extremely beautiful!

YOUNG LADY: But it wobbles; every day I put a piece
of wood under that leg, but the housemaid takes it out
when she sweeps, and I'm forced to cut a new one.
Every morning the pen holder is smudged with ink
and the inkstand too; I'm forced to wash them up after
her, every day the sun comes up. *(Pause)* What is the
worst you know?

STUDENT: Sorting laundry! Ugh!

YOUNG LADY: That is mine to do! Ugh!

STUDENT: What else!

YOUNG LADY: To be disturbed in my night's sleep,
when I must get up and refasten the catch on the
shutters...that the maid forgot.

STUDENT: What else!

YOUNG LADY: To climb a ladder and fix the damper cord after the maid has jerked it down.

STUDENT: What else!

YOUNG LADY: To sweep up after her, to dust after her, and to make the fire in the stove after her, she barely lays in the wood! To set the damper, to wipe the glasses, to set the table *over again*, uncork the bottles, open the windows, and air out, make my bed *over again*, scald the water carafe when it has gone green with scum, shop for matches and soap, which are always missing, wipe the lamp glass and trim the wicks, so that the lamps will not smoke, and so that the lamps will not go out, when there are guests I must fill them myself…

STUDENT: Sing!

YOUNG LADY: Wait! —First drudgery, drudgery that keeps life's filth away from us.

STUDENT: But you are well off, have two servants!

YOUNG LADY: That doesn't help! Even if we had three! It is exhausting to live, and I am tired at times… Think if there were a nursery too!

STUDENT: The greatest of joys…

YOUNG LADY: The costliest… Is life worth such exhaustion?

STUDENT: That all depends on the reward one wants for one's toils…I should shy away from nothing to win your hand.

YOUNG LADY: Don't talk that way! —You can never have me!

STUDENT: Why not?

YOUNG LADY: That you must never ask.

(Pause)

STUDENT: You dropped a bracelet out the window...

YOUNG LADY: Because my hand has become so thin...

(Pause)

(COOK appears with a Japanese flask in hand.)

YOUNG LADY: It is she who eats at me, and all of us.

STUDENT: What is she holding?

YOUNG LADY: It's a flask of coloring, the devil's elixir, with scorpion letters on it! It is the witch Madam Soy Sauce, that turns water into broth, that replaces gravy, that cabbage is boiled in, that turtle soup is made of.

STUDENT: Out!

COOK: You suck the marrow out of us, and we out of you; we take blood and give back water—with Coloring. This is coloring! —Now I go, but I shall stay all the same, as long as I like! *(Goes)*

(Pause)

STUDENT: Why does Bengtsson have a medal?

YOUNG LADY: To reward his great qualities.

STUDENT: Has he no faults?

YOUNG LADY: Oh yes, many great ones, but for them a man gets no medals.

(STUDENT and YOUNG LADY smile.)

STUDENT: You have many secrets here in the house...

YOUNG LADY: Like all others... Let us keep ours!

(Pause)

STUDENT: Do you love sincerity?

YOUNG LADY: Yes, in moderation!

STUDENT: There comes over me at time a raging desire to say whatever I think; but I know the world would stop altogether if men were truly sincere. *(Pause)* I went

to a funeral the other day…in church—it was most
solemn and beautiful!

YOUNG LADY: It was Chairman Hummel's?

STUDENT: My false benefactor's, yes! —At the coffin's
head stood an older friend of the deceased, and he held
the ceremonial mace; the priest especially impressed
me with his dignified bearing and his touching words.
—I wept, we all wept. —Afterwards, we went to a
tavern… There I came to know that the chief mourner
had loved the dead man's son…

(YOUNG LADY *stares, baffled by the meaning of this.*)

STUDENT: And that the deceased borrowed money
from his son's admirer… (*Pause*) The very next day the
priest was caught embezzling from the church! —Isn't
that lovely!

YOUNG LADY: Ugh!

(*Pause*)

STUDENT: You know what I think of you now?

YOUNG LADY: Don't say it, or I shall die!

STUDENT: I must, or else I'll die!…

YOUNG LADY: In asylums men say whatever they
think…

STUDENT: Absolutely right! —My father wound up in a
madhouse…

YOUNG LADY: Was he sick?

STUDENT: No, he was hale and hearty, but he was
also insane! Well, it surfaced a while ago, and under
the following circumstances… He was like all of
us surrounded by a circle of acquaintances, whom
he for short would call friends; they were a low-
minded lot, as most men are. But he had to have some
acquaintances, after all he couldn't sit by himself. Well

now, men don't say what they think of each other
in everyday life, and he didn't either. He knew well
enough how false they were, he had fathomed their
treachery to the bottom...but he was a wise man and
well brought up and so he was always polite. But one
day he threw a grand party—it was in the evening; he
was weary from the day's work, and from straining to
hold his tongue, while prattling shit with his guests...

(YOUNG LADY *winces.*)

STUDENT: Anyhow, he rapped on the dinner table
for silence, raised his glass to make a toast... Then
somehow the dam broke, and in a long tirade he
stripped them all bare, one after the other, exposing all
their falseness! Worn out, he sat down in the middle of
the table and told them all to go to hell.

YOUNG LADY: Ugh!

STUDENT: I was present, and I'll never forget what
happened next! ...Father and mother slugging away,
guests rushing for the doors...and father taken to the
madhouse where he died! *(Pause)* Keeping your mouth
shut a long time is like stagnant water that breeds rot,
and so it is in this house too. There is something rotting
here! And I thought this was paradise, when I first saw
you go in here... There I stood on a Sunday morning
and looked in; I saw a Colonel who was no colonel, I
had a noble benefactor who was a bandit and had to
hang himself, I saw a mummy who wasn't one and a
well-born spinster, by the way where is virginity to be
found? Where is beauty found? In nature and in my
own mind where it is clad in Sunday best! Where are
honor and loyalty found? In legends and children's
make-believe! Where find anything that keeps its
promise? ...In my imagination! —Now your blooms
have poisoned me and I am giving your gift back—I
begged you to accept my hand and my home, we wove

fancies, sang and played, and then the cook intruded...
*Sursum Corda! (Translator's note: Latin, "Lift up your
hearts," the opening of the Eucharist.)* Seek once more to
strike purple and fire from your golden harp...seek,
I beg, I fall to my knees... Well then, I'll do it myself!
(Takes up the harp, but the strings make no sound.) It is
deaf and dumb! To think that the loveliest blooms are
so poisonous, are the most poisonous, a curse hanging
over all creation and life...
Why were you not willing to be my bride? Because
you are sick in the well-springs of life...now I sense
the vampire in the kitchen beginning to drain me, I
think she is a Lamia who sucks the life out of children,
it is always in the kitchens that a family's children
are nipped in the bud, provided it isn't done in the
bedroom...there are poisons that steal sight, and
poisons that open eyes—I was surely born full of the
latter, for I cannot see the ugly as beautiful nor call
evil good, I cannot! Jesus Christ went down into hell,
that was his wandering on earth, the madhouse, the
pesthouse, the deathhouse, earth; and madmen killed
him, when he would free them, but the thief was let
loose, thieves always get sympathy! —Woe! Woe! unto
us all. Savior of the world save us, we perish!

(The YOUNG LADY *has shriveled into herself, seems to be
dying, she rings,* BENGTSSON *enters.)*

YOUNG LADY: Come with the screen! Quick—I die!

*(*BENGTSSON *returns with the screen, which he unfolds and
places before the* YOUNG LADY.*)*

STUDENT: The Liberator cometh! Welcome, Thou,
bland and mild! —Sleep Thou lovely, hapless, guiltless
one, suffering through no fault of thine own, sleep
dreamlessly, and when thou wakest again mayst thou
be greeted by a sun that burns not, in a home free of
dust, among friends free of shame, to a love free of

flaw... Thou wise, mild Buddha, who sits there and waits for a heaven to burgeon from earth, grant us patience in our ordeal, purify the will, that these hopes may not come to grief!

(There is a soughing in the strings of the harp; the room fills with a white light.)

STUDENT: The sun saw I, to me it seemed
That I beheld the one concealed
And all his works were for man's joy,
blessèd be he that doeth good.
for deeds committed in thy wrath
cannot be recompensed by evil;
comfort him thou hast distrest
with thy goodness, thou shalt be repaid.
Naught to fear hath he who does no ill:
Goodness is innocence.

(A wailing is heard from behind the screen.)

STUDENT: You wretched little child, child of this delusive, guilt-ridden, suffering and deadly world; this ever varying, disappointing and painful world! The Lord of Heaven grant you mercy for your faring...

(The room vanishes; Boecklin's Isle of the Dead *takes shape in the background; music, faint, still, pleasantly melancholy, is heard from the island.)*

END OF PLAY